For Everywoman

A Collection of Poetry To Explore Our
Complicated Relationship With Food and
Our Bodies

Julie Mast

BookLeaf
Publishing

India | USA | UK

Dedication

To my grandmas, my mama, my sister, my daughters, my roomies, my girlfriends...if we bottled up all the power we put behind thinking of our bodies...we could have moved mountains. Here's to not letting one more ounce of power getting taken from us. We are all meant for so much more.

Preface

My eating disorder started with a tiny little lump of fat
that settled under my butt cheeks when I first started to
get hips. Reflecting on it now, it seems so silly to think of
how that little ounce of adipose tissue threw me into a
tailspin that left me with dangerously low body fat and
disordered thinking about food and my body. But what
was most harmful was my feeling of being so alone with
my obsessive secret world within.

This book of poems reflects how I felt, how I think many
women feel and also how I overcame it. Although I
consider myself healed, the thoughts still find a way to
creep their way in. But now I know well the critic's voice
and I can pretty quickly shut her up...no room for her in
my life anymore. She can lead to self-loathing faster than
anyone else could...in a half a heartbeat.

I hope you find these poems healing and that in some
way they make you feel understood and heard. We are
all alone with our thoughts, and when they turn to our
body image, they can spiral and get dark quickly. I also
hope you find a way out of this thinking...a little tiny key
to the door to freedom. It's lovely on the other side, the
air is pure and clean and there isn't any room for shame,
deprivation or despair.

Acknowledgements

Thank you to my angels, who so many years ago helped me to truly surrender my eating disorder. It paved the way for a lifetime of surrender and trust in the Divine.

1. A Note To Men

Thousands of questions rattled around her head before you heard this one slip from her mouth,
"Do I look fat in these pants?"
All you hear is the question that corners and confuses you...but there's so much more.
10 times more.
1,000 times more.
10,000 times 10,000 more.
So many questions she's asked herself and lies she's repeated to herself.
Again and again.

"I'm too pathetic to be seen."
"I'm too fat to show up, everyone will stare."
"Why is my body betraying me?"
"My arms are too flabby to wear short sleeves."
"Why can't I stop eating?"
"Why can't I exercise more?"
"I'm ashamed. I'm laughable. I'm never going to win this war."

The bargaining, the comparison, the self-hatred...all so loud in her head.
So you hear, "Do I look fat in these pants?'

You squirm, you laugh inside....but some advice:
Don't say a word.
Look at her with fierce, fierce love and wrap her up in it.
Let her know her worth was never in her weight.

2. The Ride

The ride, or the run or the crazed circuit.
You are in a war against an enemy that's impossible to
pin down.
The extra pinch in your waist as you button up.
The tug of your blouse sleeve where it feels like it may
be too tight.
The extra tiny lump in your hip curve that screams at
you when you turn in the mirror.
Physically it's hard to hunt and find and measure the
enemy collecting on your frame.
Mentally, nothing is more clear.
More fat equals
loss of power,
loss of appeal,
loss of esteem,
loss of worth.
So you keep on running, riding, lifting like you are at
war, punching ghosts.
But no one ever wins, ever.
Wave your white flag..for your anger or will can't
permanently dissolve it.
Seek peace. Seek freedom from the fight.

3. So Unfair

A fat man, on stage.
A business suit.
A lecture.
An audience who is captivated by the subject, by the man who knows his stuff.
Little thought is diverted to weight, but not distracting.
He's intelligent, he has command of the room.
They think, maybe his wife is a good cook? Perhaps a few well-deserved bourbons after work?
How could he ever have time to exercise anyway?

A fat woman, on stage.
A business suit.
A lecture.
An audience who is captivated by the subject, by a woman who knows her stuff.
Much thought is diverted to her weight. It's distracting.
She's intelligent, but clearly no self-control. She doesn't hold the power in the room.
Maybe she likes her food and indulges her insatiable appetite. Clearly not happy inside.
Why can't she at least find the time to exercise?

4. Knock Knock

Knock Knock...
Who's there?
Food.
Food who?
Food Everywhere. All. The. Time.
Food in the wee morning hours before anyone is up.
What meal can I skip today? I can feel my belly rolls.
Food as your feet touch the ground from your bed. What can I eat for breakfast that will zero out with my exercise?
Food as you fix your breakfast. Do I really need two pieces of toast?
Food as you get ready for work. These pants are so tight in the waist. Did I gain weight yesterday? What did I eat?
Food as you are driving. What should I order at lunch? If I order a salad, people will think I'm dieting.
Food as you walk in to your desk. Was Mary really eating a bagel? Bagel and a size 2?
Food as you walk by the break room. Who brought donuts? Don't do it, don't smell, don't cave, walk by.
Food as you bend down to pee. I can feel my fat roll on my leg. No dinner tonight.
Food as you sit down for lunch. I don't know what to

order. No dinner tonight, so let's go big at lunch.

Food as you leave for home. Why did I eat so much at lunch and why am I hungry?

Food as you walk in your door. What snacks do I have?

Food as you watch TV. The ice cream is chirping at me. The chips are chirping at me. The wine is really chirping...

Food as you get ready for bed. I hate myself. I ate too much. I want one more tiny scoop. Just a little bite.

Food as you fall asleep. What should I fix for breakfast? Will I even be hungry by then? I want frozen waffles.

Food in the middle of the night. Oh my gosh..how many calories did I even eat yesterday? Too soon for a waffle? Repeat. Repeat. Repeat.

5. Coloring Outside the Lines

My body has colored outside the lines.
A good girl stays small, doesn't take up much room.
Stays within her tight curves and never has an appetite
for more.
Doesn't lose control, eats when she's hungry, stops when
she's full.
All seems so simple, these rules of staying in the lines.
But my body has colored outside the lines.
This should be a victory of nonconformity.
Drawing a tree purple and a frog pink.
Instead, there's shame.
Loss of agency.
Loss of worth.
When can coloring outside the lines
just be seen as original and natural?
New and enlightened lines...where normal comes in all
sizes.

6. Heavy

Heavy has nothing to do with a number on the scale.

Heavy is my heart. It aches for freedom.

Heavy is my mind. It's filled with a thousand thoughts.

Heavy is my spirit. It feels dark and lonely.

Heavy is my burden. I'm at war, and there is less and less of me to share.

Heavy is the darkness that I am carrying.

All day, everyday, every minute and every second.

I am carrying the darkness of shame.

It's heavy.

7. To Everywoman

To Everywoman..
From so early on
we have been told
you are
too..
(you can fill in the blanks with
a thousand things).
If not from the lips
of your parents, family
or friends
then from the shoutings
of a society who gives
power to the perfect.
For all the little girls, the teens,
the young adults, the new moms, the
the middle agers, the new
grandmas...
it's time to set ourselves free.
Time to take the baby steps
to healing our relationship
with our sweet, miracle-filled
bodies.

8. Light

From the outside...I'm heavy. I'm fat. I've gone beyond.
But inside, I hold onto so much more heavy.
Thoughts of inadequacy and shame
weigh heavier than the scale.
My heart is heavy, my never taken paths are heavy,
My showing up with a smile and faked confidence feels
oh so heavy.
I'm ready for light with a capital "L".
Light to come in and shake me all up inside.
Light to come in and show me no matter how heavy I
feel,
I am eternally Light.

9.

9. Freedom

Remember how freedom tasted?
It was so long ago...can you remember?
When the only C-word you cared about was Cake,
Not Calories, Cellulite or Calculations?
Let me remind you....
It was running through the sprinklers, green grass and
water....
Never thinking about how you looked in your swimsuit.
It was before "bad" and "good" for you...
You never tagged shame on a donut.
It was bare feet on hot cement,
Running to catch the ice-cream man.
It was being so engrossed in something,
You would forget to eat.
Your body's natural rhythms ruled the day.
It was a mind and heart free
From the tethers of fear.
Fear of fat,
Fear of too much,
Fear of losing the battle.
Freedom tastes so good.

10. Dear Mind

Dear Mind,

I am a miracle.

You've spoken so harshly to me, I sense so much anger.

I understand you think I'm not listening.

But I am.

You've told me thousands of times I am fat...

So just making your thoughts come true.

But I'm not writing to call you out..just asking you for a peace offering.

But first, I have to know....

Why do you not trust me?

When did I become the enemy?

When did you stop finding joy in our running, skipping and jumping?

I am a miracle.

Trillions of cells, reactions, breaths, synapses, heart beats, neurons firing..

All so you can walk upright around this beautiful world.

But you hate me, think I've betrayed you.

Can we start over?

I am a miracle.

And so are you.

With your bright, intelligent and creative mind and my strong, capable and wise body...

We can create miracles *together.*

I never stopped taking care of you and loving you.

Trust me.

Love,

Your Body

11. The Weight Fairy

What if...
A fairy came down and all you could be
was the exact weight that you currently see?
Would you want to curl up and never
come out of your cave?
Would you forever find ways to
be small and not make any waves?
Could you imagine a life beyond the
dream size never attained?
Could you be bolder and braver
and feel like you are living unchained?
Who would you be?
Could you find deep peace knowing
you couldn't change?
Would you find your purpose and joy
In this known range?
Who would you be precious child..
Find and love her now,
And your heart will be set free and wild.

12. And

I give you permission precious woman,
To feel flabby **and** creative
To feel overweight **and** brilliant.
To feel pudgy **and** empowered.
To feel heavy **and** grateful.
To feel fleshy **and** kind.
To feel stout **and** capable.
To feel large **and** luminous.
The world needs *your* ands.
Don't let them hide within you.

13. Brilliant Body

My body is strong,
My body is wise,
It is incomparable to any other human.
My body is a spiritual chemical reactor.
My body holds light, energy and action.
It is a walking miracle.
My body is ever-changing.
My body is always working towards balance.
It is brilliant.

15. The Circle

18

When we gather in this sacred circle,
We speak of diets, weight and food.
Membership requires us to be unhappy in our forms,
It's what bonds us, we travel heavy in this world,
together.
If I have no body problems to solve, what would I say?
With every pound I shed, I back step out of
This community of broken sisters.
With a fit and healthy body, I will be abandoning our
pact..
To belong, I must stay stuck.

16. Brave

Are you brave enough?
To be thin...to be free of excuses?
I can't dance because people will stare at my fat roll over
my dress.
I won't go swimming until I fit into my size ten suit.
I won't play with my kids in this tired and hefty body.
Are you brave enough to live in a world of yes instead
of...
I'll wait until?
Imagine you have arrived, living in your dream weight...
Are you brave enough to live there? To thrive there?
To step up and actually live up to
all the promises you made?

17. Red Bikini 1

The sun kissed my sixteen year old nose,
that was poking out under my oversized shades...
all topped off with my big cotton candy pink smile.
I run into the waves.
Knowing my round bum barely bounced and the boys
and men were noticing me.
Muscles taking center stage in front of what should have
been a little flab.
So proud of my little red bikini and how it showed off
My hard-earned eight pack tummy.
Freedom, splashes, attention, laughter on the outside.
The cost of my little red bikini was
calculations, hours on the treadmill, obsession and
loneliness.
On the inside, I was at war with an enemy that never
slept.

18. Red Bikini 2

21

Retired red bikini, hibernating at the depths of my
drawer.
Waiting for summer, when I can show off my tight body
at the shore.
The little red bikini should be fun and care free,
But instead it taunts and is constantly challenging me.
Telling me I'm way too fat and those thin days are gone.
You aren't worth anything if you aren't a size one.
Little red bikini, there were too many times I didn't obey.
I wish you would fit my body just as it is,
 or kindly go away.

19. Little Birdie

Sweet little birdie, remember the freedom to fly?
Where you could just spread your sweet wings
and go anywhere you please?
But now you are tethered to this cage of construct.
The door is firmly locked.
You are stuck in these bars of shame
and questions of why you don't hold a certain shape.
Sweet little birdie, you were never meant to be caged.
You can't all be just one shape or one size.
If all the birdies had to be perfect to fly, this world would
be
So barren. So quiet.
So break free little birdie, fly with all your might.
The world needs all the beautiful birdies to spread their
wings
and take flight.

20. Catching Thoughts

If I had a net to catch every little thought,
that every single woman
had in one minute,
across the
world
about food,
about weight or body.
I would catch a storm, a force so great.
If I could turn it to love, the world would
be healed. In an instant. Just like that.

21. Step Into You

Let her go...
The tired, the weak, the one who has been beaten up
over
every wrong choice
and every single extra pound.
Let her go...
She no longer serves the woman you are becoming.
You are exquisite. You are brilliant.
Not time for weight, no time for small thoughts.
Your cells are aligning perfectly to bring your natural
shape to the show.
You are at the front of the stage, ready to shine.
You are finally dropping everything that doesn't serve
you becoming...
perfectly YOU.